Transcendent Light

a collection of feelings that transpired
through healing

Kristina Rocks

/ BookLeaf
Publishing

India | USA | UK

Made with ❤ on the BookLeaf Publishing Platform

www.bookleafpub.in

www.bookleafpub.com

Dedication

To the people and animals that have shown me love, care, and patience. I wouldn't be here without you.

Preface

any of the thoughts & feelings I've shared within these pages should serve as mere glimpses of a much larger kaleidoscope of emotions. bringing these to life, and preparing a physical database in which to process my life and future has been so truly healing to me. thank you for reading along with me.

Acknowledgements

I must admit, I was far too shy to have anyone help me with this project. So I'd like to formally acknowledge how much I appreciate you, <u>the reader,</u> in having an interest in this book and for being someone to share it with. I hope this collection of poems brings about as much thought and healing as they did for me while writing them.

1. the before

There are places
that people go
ages of peace and safety
that they can return to
and visit
'the before'

I am not
have never been
and never will be one of those travelers

and that is
forever the greatest
loss of my life

2. the mask

Who am I without this mask of safety
I grew it myself from the very beginning, a brilliant
design born of a 5 year old in danger

I've worn it with pride ever since
Like a battle scar —
for this shield is the reason
I made it out alive

I like to think that one day I'll be able to remove it
Like wiping away your foundation at the end of the day

Relief
But also a gentle reminder of who you are without it

3. the beloved

A lighthouse guides a ship back to shore, warns of the cliffs looming

A safe welcoming for all aboard

A lighthouse —as a lover— looks out into the vast darkness and guides the beloved home

Piercing light illuminates at times the very worst,
Still our unconditional devotion safeguards a warm belonging

4. the quiet

I wonder what it was like to be my mother

She always says she tried her best, I know that for
certain

But what did it do to her,
to hear my crying,
trapped in telephone lines running through the city

every other weekend and every Wednesday evening

What about that one long summer? Right before high
school? She was out of reach, in a failed attempt for a
warmer life

I was alone for 2 weeks,enjoying the quiet safety for
myself
and my velvet eared, white-tipped tail companion

Danger was held astray for us both,
until he came home to check on the dishes and laundry

A few plates destroyed in my direction, a few drawers of
laundry dumped out above me

I wonder if she ever felt a maternal urge to come back
and save me?

I wonder if she ever felt a disheartening relief
that *she* was still safe?

5. the goodbye

Safety has always arrived in the smallest of glimmers
Unrecognizable to the human eye and unfamiliar to
those who need it the most

Today, safety marks a measurable distance between
where I've been and where I am
Still sad, mad, and alone
But now those feelings are encompassed by an invisible
net

Holding me together like a layer of skin I've never quite
had

Here, space is created for me and feelings are received
with encouragement and kindness

With practice I can build this space for myself, but for
now I must pause in this self-exploration until another
entrusted arrives

I promise not to fall behind in the progress I've made, I
promise to keep trying
with both courage & curiosity

"Gratitude" is not enough to express what is left here in your absence
What remains is a recognition of safety and the desire to meet it more often

I look forward to the conversations I'll have with anger, fear, sadness, and judgement
And appreciate the one who taught me to listen to their stories

This is not goodbye, it's simply talk to you later

6. the monster

My mind holds a home filled with memories
I don't know why, they don't have reason
I know not why they are mine to hold.

A bedroom, that looks like the solar system.
Stars, planets, black holes and supernovas. It makes you
feel small, and helps you remember that nothing here is
actually real.

I have a kitchen, it's spotless and empty.
All marble counter tops and sky lights
It's unlived and sterile, food has never touched that
fridge
I think this is where the food insecurity lives

In the living room is every friend I've ever loved
Which fortunately means all of them, in one place
Forever laughing, dancing, with breezy open windows
and sunset splashed across the walls

The study feels grand, because it's floor to ceiling
bookcases, dimly lit chandeliers and candelabras
And it's filled with every story I've ever escaped to

It's easy to think the attic is my favorite, with an easel to
express every emotion I've never been allowed to voice
There's paint splattered on the floor, and on the walls
Pastels and dried acrylic roses painted on every surface
I will make this beautiful

I will not dare to speak of what memories live within my
basement
The ones that send me running up the stairs, as soon as I
flick the lights off
Wondering what monster will catch my ankles today

7. the day

To be born the day of Imbolic means that I should be a hope for easier days to come

I am halfway between the darkest nights of winter and the sunrise of spring

I am a lit flame on the precipice of a hopeful soon

Renewed light that leads to a gentle embrace, strength to hold on for just a little while longer

You will hear the birds again, and feel the warm air

You will grow into your new self and the new year with grace

8. the body

I have not written in 2 months

I am alone and do not wish the recount the cathartic act
of slicing my hair off at 4 and 10 years

Nor do I wish to explore
how that memory is a reminder of all the things my
childhood lacked
Bodily autonomy and safety to name a few

Hair holds memory, but so do skin and teeth.

At 30, with far less hair, how far have I gotten with this
last 16 years of puppeteering?

If you'd ask me, I could tell you I've reached a desolate
finish line

Still, I've finished last

9. the skin

What is it like being a quarter Lakota?
Well, my lack of melanin makes me look like an
imposter
It makes me feel like one too

The feeling of not enough comes to mind

Not *far* enough to experience a childhood that was free
from inter generational trauma and abuse

Not *close* enough to not be mistaken for a yt liberal with
a savior complex or someone with a great great grandma
who was "a Cherokee princess"

I spend all of my time learning, researching, reading
about a culture and heritage that I'm not comfortable
sharing about myself

I want to belong to my family,
I want my family to belong to me

10. the cycle

Hear me out
Is there ever an excuse to have kids for a selfish reason?
To replay the storyline with a different ending

It ends with unconditional love
Belonging

Abuse, trauma and neglect are things they've heard
about
But they get to win the lottery on having the best dad of
all time

We're breaking cycles here

When you're married to the most kind and loving person
to exist,
It's hard to not picture the redemption arch you can
provide to the kids

I've never felt safety, love, care before you
unconditionally chose me

I walked the planet for 23 years *without*

The love you've given me transcends our relationship,
and is something I will never not give to myself
I've learned how to value, protect and unconditionally
love me (most days) due to your example

I will never be able to thank you enough
So, let's pass it on.

11. the question

You ask me

Do you want to stay here with your dad or come with me?

As a highly perceptive and empathetic child, I looked around and tried to understand

Who I could help, who I could hurt

At 5 years old I was smart enough to know that if I stayed dad would stop crying

At 25 years old you should have known if it wasn't safe for you, it wasn't safe for me

12. the feeling

I understand a persons desire
To find ones purpose through career, income, and
success
A greater understanding of the role you play in this
simulation
Of how you *should* interact with the NPC's around you

I do <u>not</u> understand how that is ever enough to satisfy
what we really yearn for,
Feeling alive
Feeling loved
Feeling real

It is never enough for me.

13. the preconceived

I really did believe that finding you would change my life
I thought it would be bring me a built in support system
that I wouldn't doubt or second guess
Someone I had been for others but could never find for
myself

He took so many things from me, and even now
He takes,
He takes,
He takes.

It took me two years to understand, that while it's your
decision to make
The decision was based in what had already been stolen
from you and yours

And through those preconceived notions
He steals from me,

An older sister
A niece and nephew
A first impression

14. the being

I do not know how to immortalize something in writing
that I hold so much fear and acknowledgement of
eventually leaving me

The first *being* I was not afraid to love, and who showed
me I could be as gentle and loving as you

My polka dot dog, as my great Aunt Ruby says
I find myself collecting trinkets and art
Portraits and jewelry, all made with you in mind

What otherwise feels like the embodiment of a
Dalmatian

As if that would allow me to hold onto you any longer,
than our shared future decides

Heart + soul, you've left imprints in the shape of spots in
every part of my life and mind
From childhood dreams to healing the child within

Thank god herself for bringing someone so loyal and
loving
Thank god herself for many, many more years to come

15. the favorite

It may sound harsh, but often I feel:

I am someone that nobody cares about at any significant
level
I am not anyone's favorite person
Never somebody's number one

I am not the favorite child
I am not the favorite sibling, nor aunt, nor niece
I am not the favorite colleague, nor employee, nor
student
Not even the favorite of any one friend

I am filler to those around me with existing *and
exceptional* favorites, with whom I could never compete

I am lonely

16. the homecoming

Akin to little fires

Between the volcanos and the sound, down below a sea of green

No matter the weather, the lights of homes and families flicker between the towering conifers

I am grateful to have this homecoming

and acknowledge more than ever the importance of caring for this land and people

17. the decision

I've been told we met when I was 8, though I don't recall
our first encounter
I was weary of most people's grandparents, most of all
my own
I didn't have a relationship that was safe and secure with
my parents, let alone someone else's

I'm still not sure why you immediately chose to love me
In an unconditional way—
Your warmth and caring nature was what I always
craved *but never trusted*

I had never had someone love me before without
something in return,
Someone that showed up for every chorus concert and
band recital
Someone who always kept photos of me in her home,
from every holiday, from every school year
Someone who loved me even though I was not of their
own flesh and blood

She made the choice to love me for me, as unrelated and
tyrannical as I was
As much as she did her other grandchildren

Without a second thought given

I keep your photo up in my home,
I wait for your call on every birthday

and I hope to be able to tell you one day, that I'm relieved
you filled the gap in which two women decided against

18. the cruel

If you want to know a secret,
I'd be happy to share one with you

I could have forgiven what you did to me
Physically, emotionally
All the "you stole my childhood from me" things you put
me through

<u>But I will never forgive what you did to her.</u>

I will wait for you to die, for your cold body to return to
the earth,
before I could even begin to think about giving you the
opportunity to be forgiven.

I will hold myself back from that peace, if that means I
can hold you from it even farther

Because there is no crueler punishment than dying
alone, and that is exactly what you gave and what you
deserve.

19. the protector

You often remind me that I am my mother's child
That if given the chance, I also wouldn't have been able
to prevent or stop the things that happened to myself (no
matter the age)

I am my mothers child because I've made the same
mistakes,
Taken the same course of action

Not a mother to a human, but to my angel baby Rose

And while I didn't know about our tradition then,
your name still somehow became yours because of the
long line of mothers
to my mother
And the cells that have been carried down, and live
within me

I am my mother's child because through you I have
learned
to have humility, because I am imperfect
to be patient, because I can be chaotic too

I am my mother's child, because fear has set me back

You are your mother's child, because through our fear
you protect

20. the friend

8.5 years apart makes a big difference,
Sometimes I wonder if we'd still be this close if we were
closer in age

As we've grown together,
It has been difficult to imagine all the things I've missed
out on
as an only child for so long before you

It wasn't asked of me, but I took it on willingly
To safeguard a safe place for you

To look after you, as if you were mine to do that for
I believed I had to save you in ways I had wished for
myself

I look back at those moments, sometimes with regret
and sometimes with nostalgia

As you've grown, you've become someone I can lean on
instead of carry
Not to say I didn't enjoy holding you

But this is what it feels like to be sisters

Friends
A trusted source of advice, and honest feedback

This is what it means to protect,
and to be protected

As I've grown,
I now understand that we can face anything together
and find comfort in our shared past.

21. the end

I hope every beginning ends with us

After every cold morning and long day we didn't want,
leads us back wrapped in each others limbs
willing to do it all again.

I hope every trip ends with us at home, unpacking and
settling in for the mundane together

And every dreary Spring that brings us tulips and false
hope for warmth,
leads us right back to our Douglas fir winters

I hope in every universe, every timeline, every
dimension and version

ends with us,
here together

www.ingramcontent.com/pod-product-compliance
Lightning Source LLC
Chambersburg PA
CBHW051000030426
42339CB00007B/416